FIRST GRAPHICS | BODY SYSTEMS

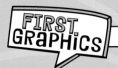

A Tour of Your Respiratory System

by Mary Reina
illustrated by Chris B. Jones

CONSULTANT:
MARJORIE J. HOGAN, MD
ASSOCIATE PROFESSOR OF PEDIATRICS AND PEDIATRICIAN
UNIVERSITY OF MINNESOTA AND HENNEPIN COUNTY MEDICAL CENTER
MINNEAPOLIS, MINNESOTA

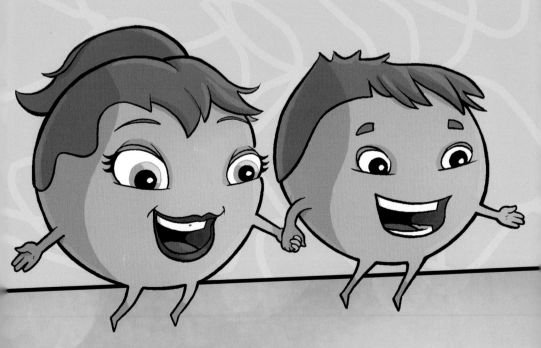

CAPSTONE PRESS
a capstone imprint

First Graphics are published by Capstone Press,
1710 Roe Crest Drive, North Mankato, Minnesota 56003.
www.capstonepub.com

Library of Congress Cataloging-in-Publication Data
Reina, Mary.
  A tour of your respiratory system / by Mary Reina ; illustrated by Chris B. Jones.
    p. cm.—(First graphics. Body systems)
  Summary: "In graphic novel format, follows Molly and Ollie Oxygen as they
travel through and explain the workings of the human respiratory system"—
Provided by publisher.
  Includes bibliographical references and index.
  ISBN 978-1-4296-8652-5 (library binding)
  ISBN 978-1-4296-9330-1 (paperback)
  ISBN 978-1-62065-265-7 (ebook PDF)
  1. Respiratory organs—Juvenile literature. I. Jones, Chris B., ill. II. Title.
  QM251.R45 2013   2011051829
  611'.2—dc23

Editor: Christopher L. Harbo
Designer: Lori Bye
Art Director: Nathan Gassman
Production Specialist: Kathy McColley

Printed in the United States of America in Stevens Point, Wisconsin.
032012   006678WZF12

Table of Contents

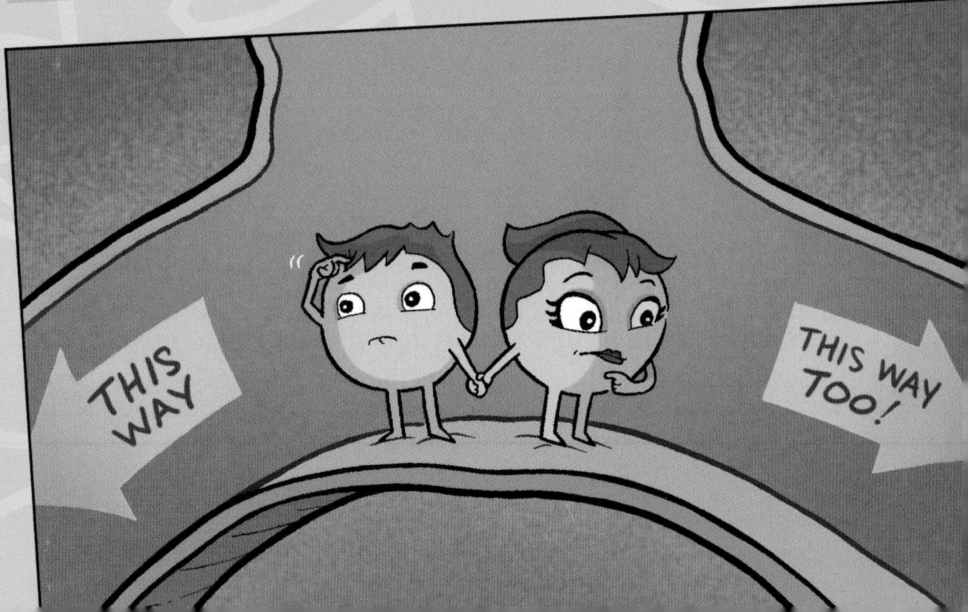
THIS WAY
THIS WAY TOO!

Taking It All In

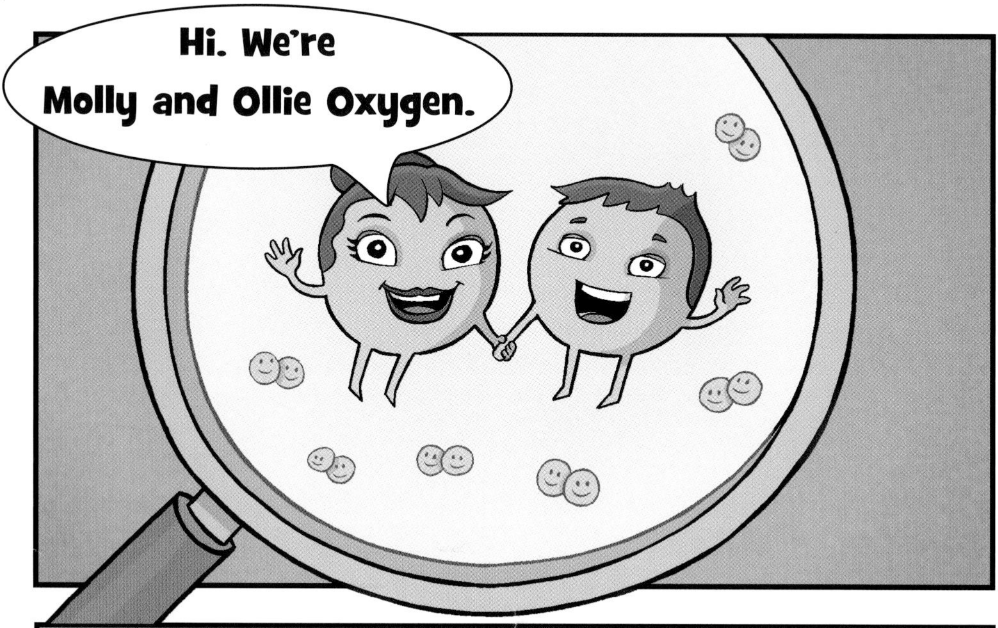
Hi. We're
Molly and Ollie Oxygen.

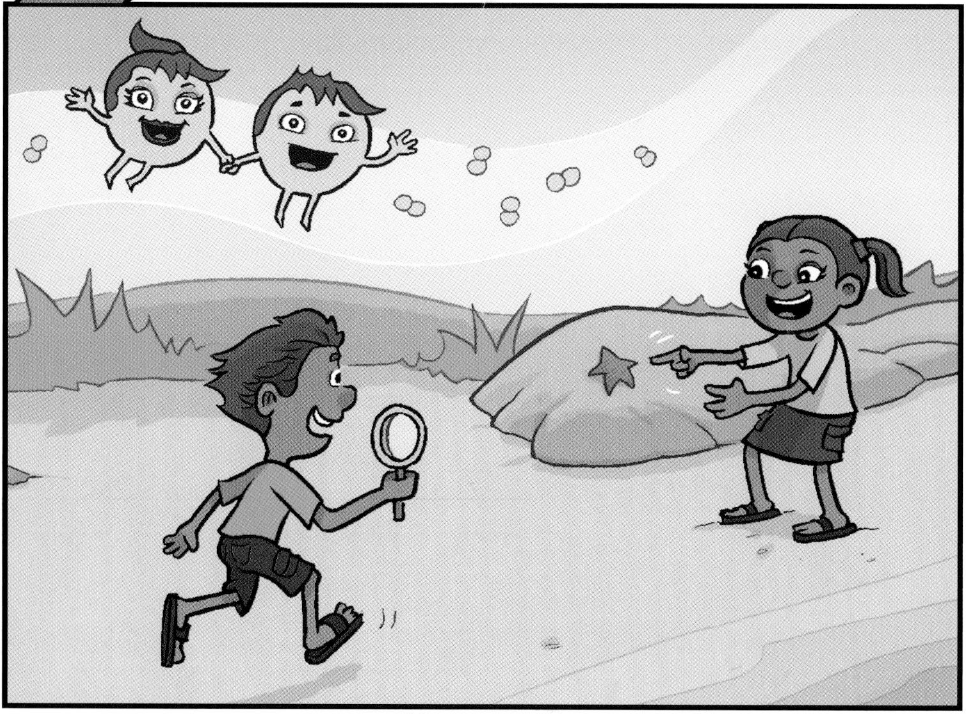

We're a gas in the air you breathe.

Oxygen keeps you alive. It enters your body through the respiratory system.

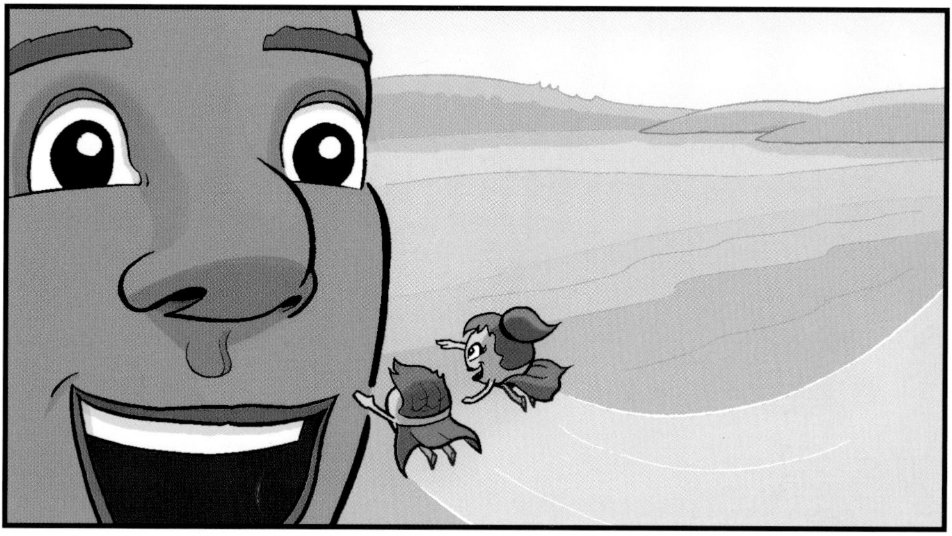

This system of airways lets you breathe in and out.

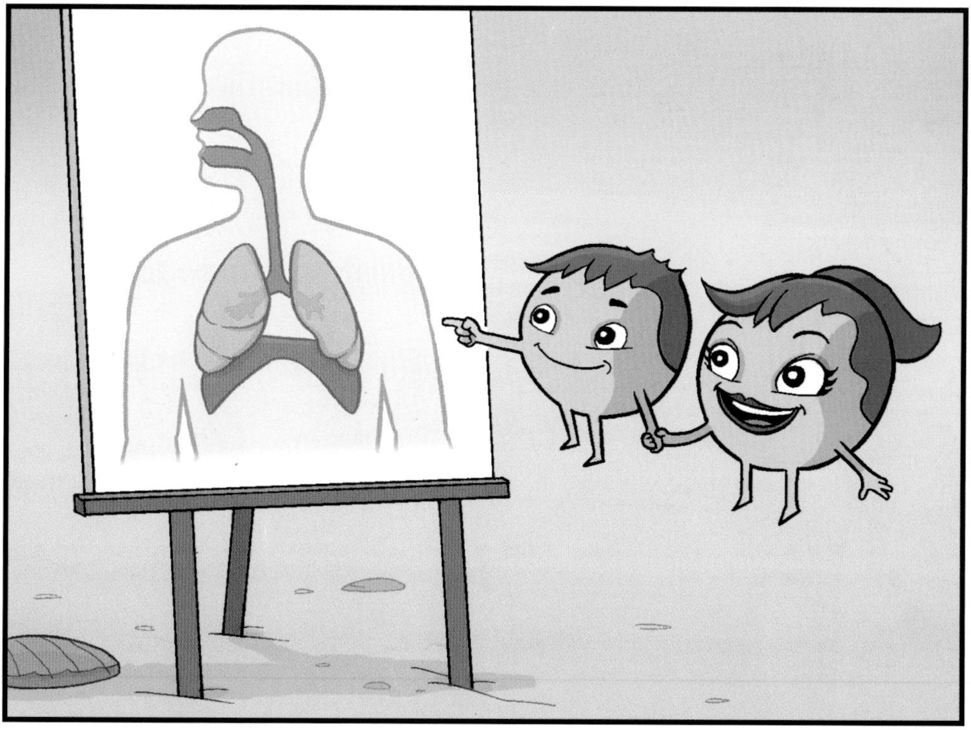

The respiratory system brings air to your lungs.

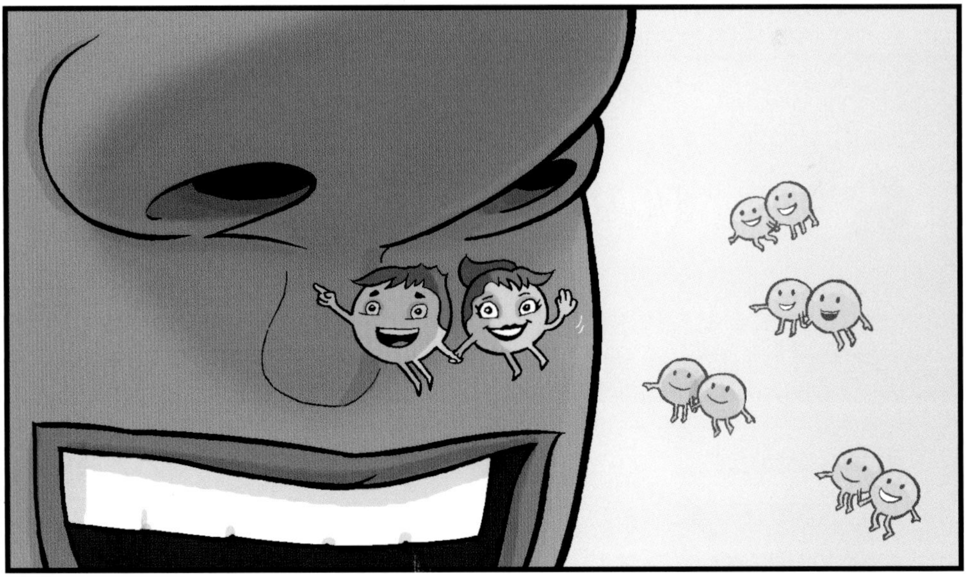

When you breathe in, a wall of muscle called the diaphragm pulls down.

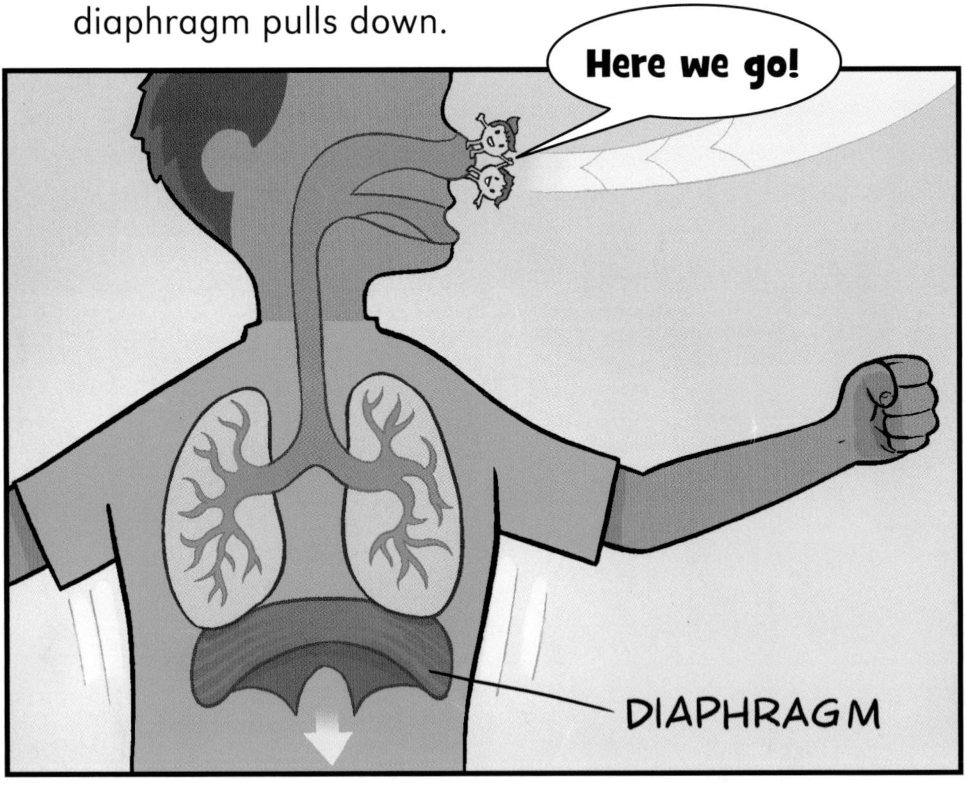
Here we go!
DIAPHRAGM

This movement lets air flow into your body.

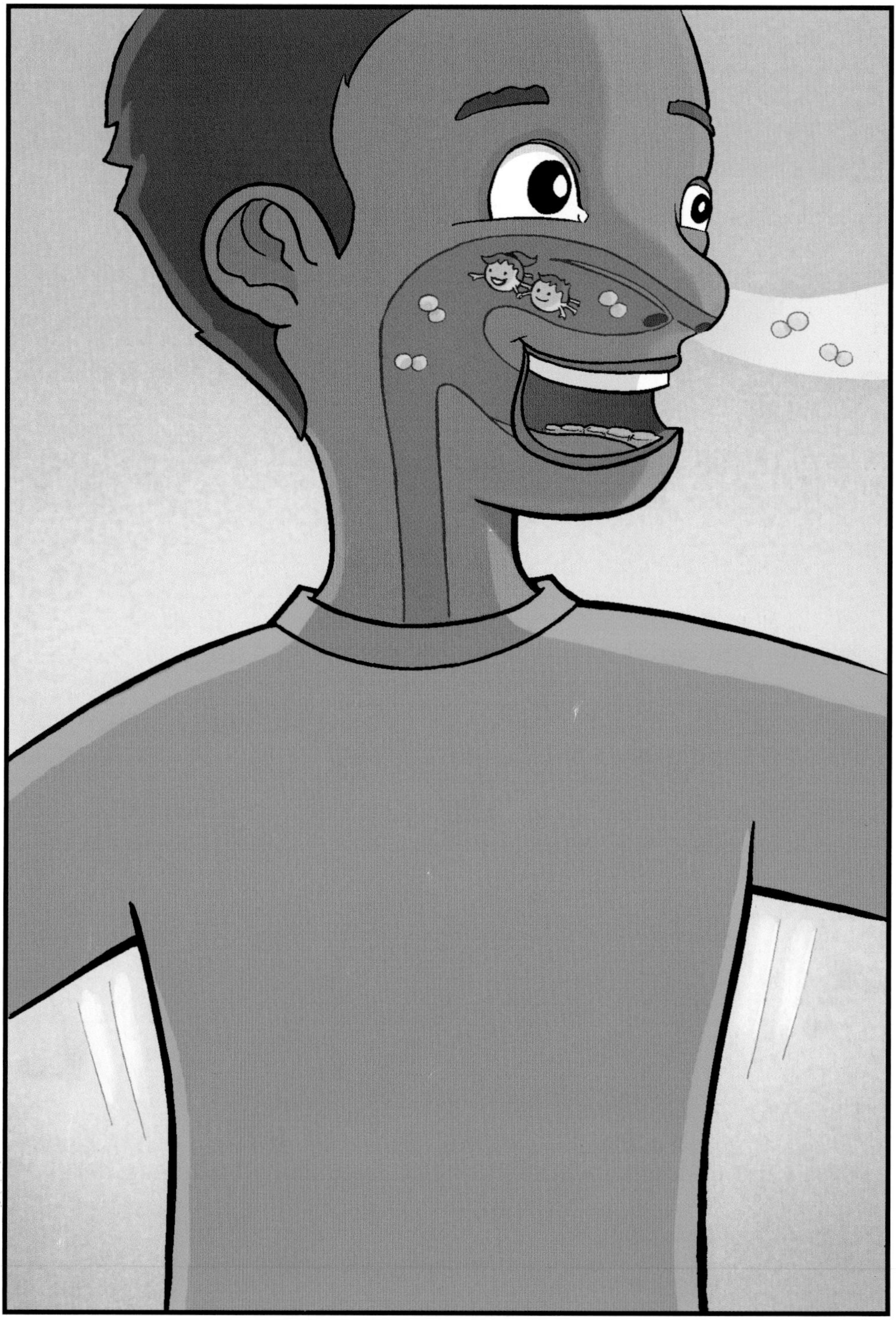

Your nose cleans and warms the air.

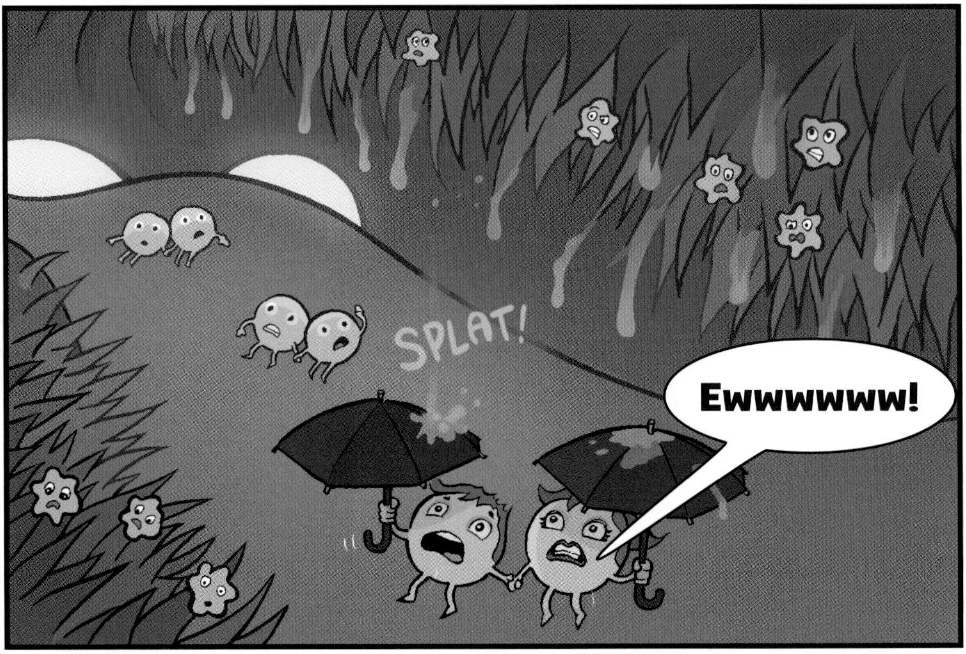
SPLAT!
Ewwwwww!

Then the air flows into the throat. It passes through a long airway called the trachea.

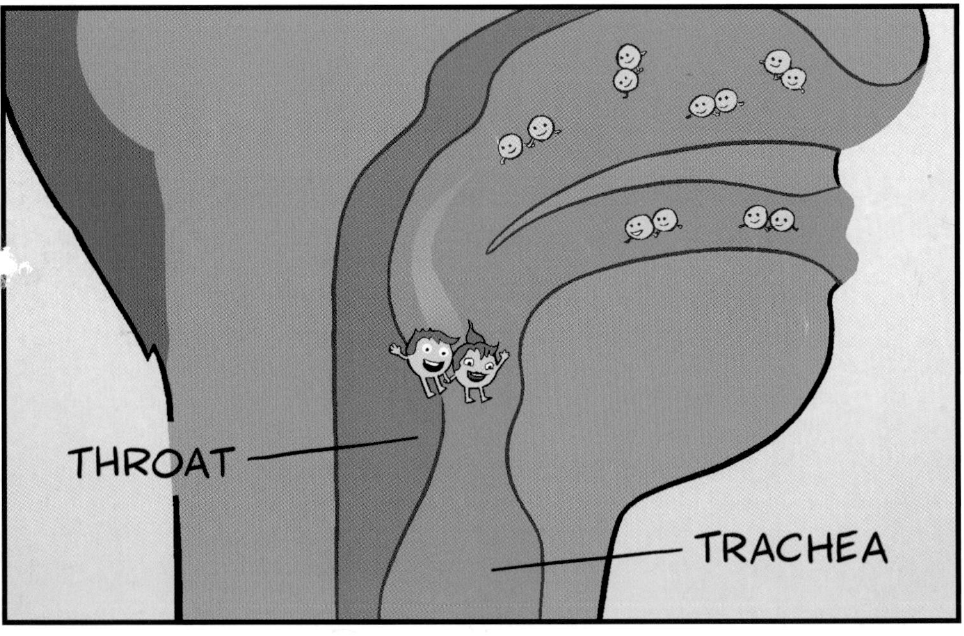
THROAT
TRACHEA

The trachea splits into two tubes called bronchi.

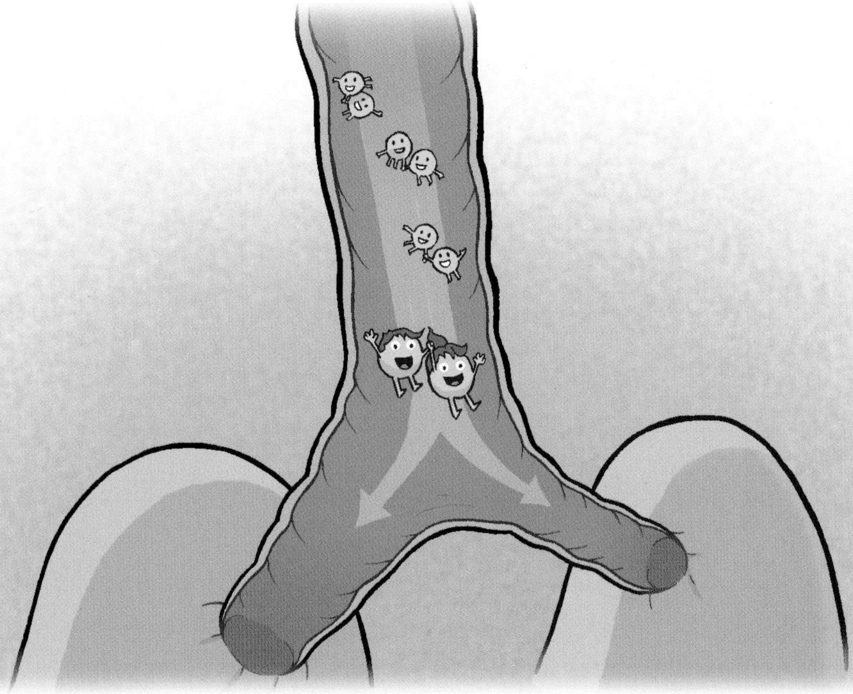

Each of the bronchi lets air into the lungs.

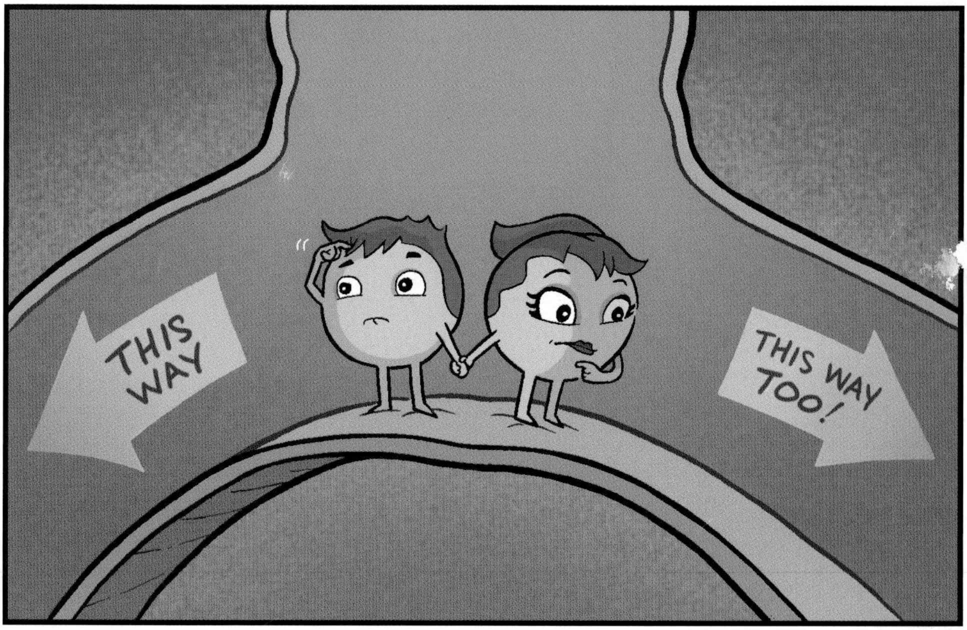
THIS WAY
THIS WAY TOO!

Going Places

Inside the lungs, the bronchi branch into smaller tubes called bronchioles.

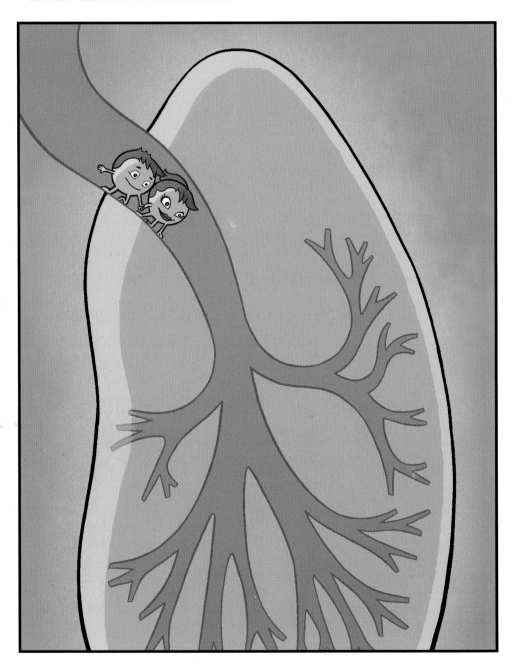

As the lungs swell, air reaches the bronchioles.

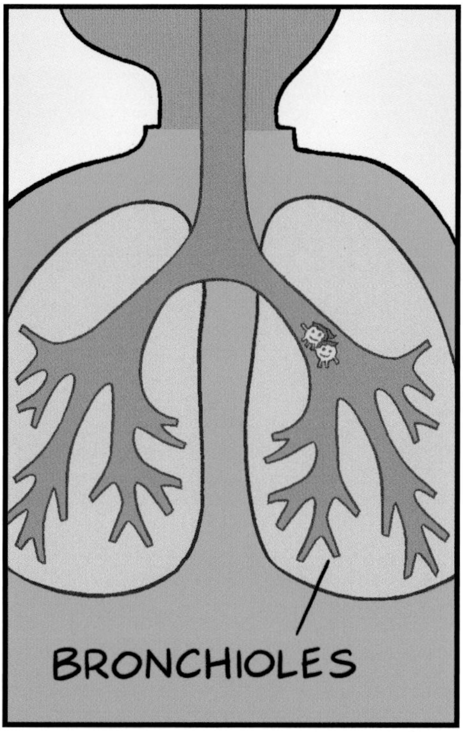
BRONCHIOLES

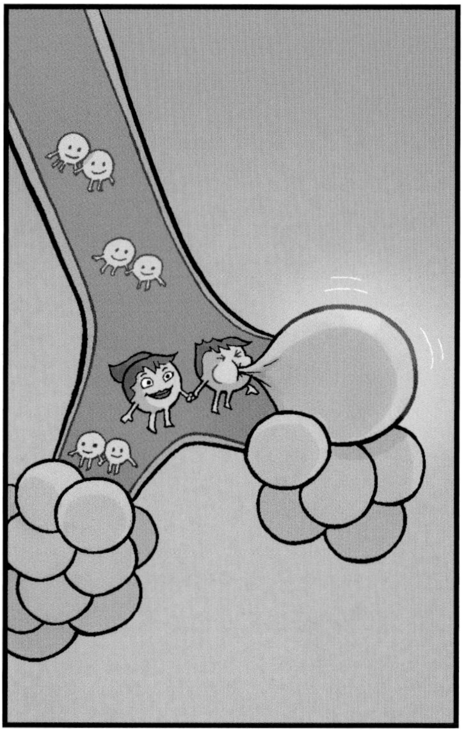

Many air sacs cover the ends of these tiny tubes.

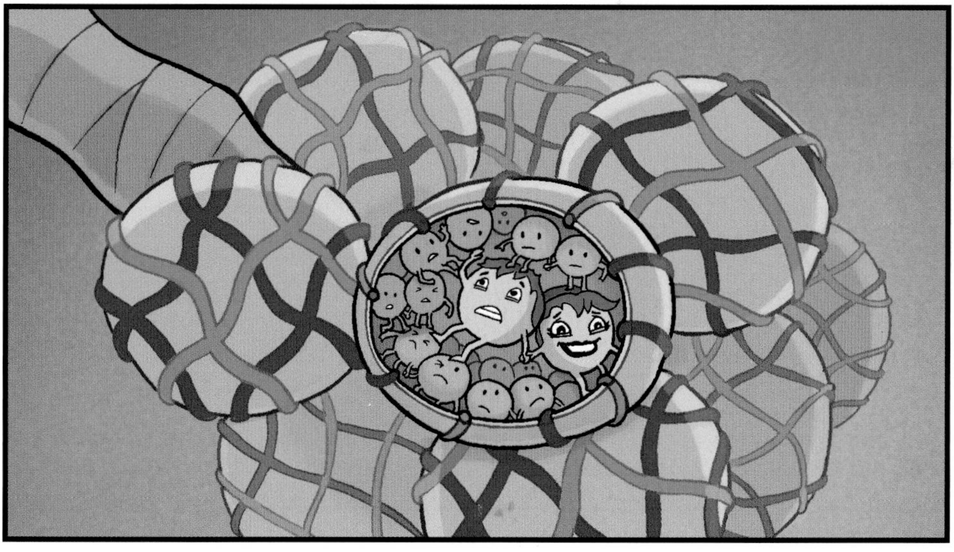

Every air sac is covered by a net of capillaries.

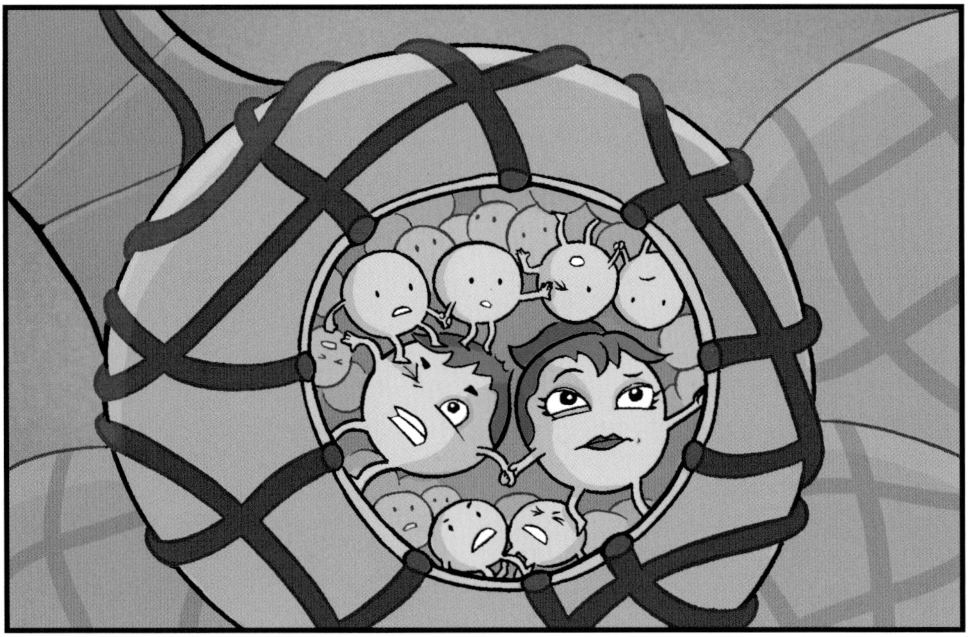

Capillaries are tiny tubes that carry blood.

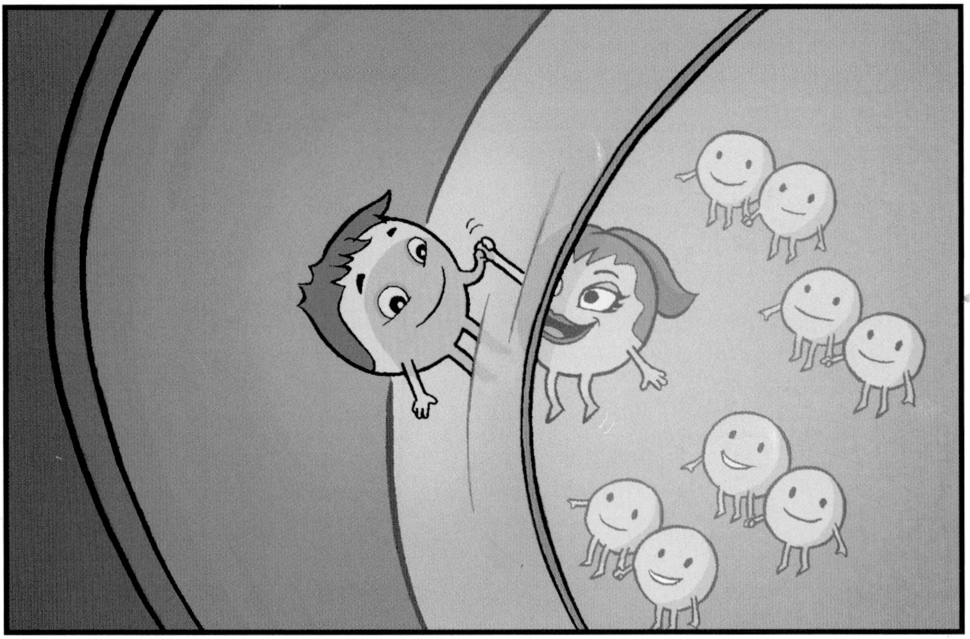

They have thin walls that let oxygen pass right through them.

Oxygen attaches to red blood cells inside the capillaries.

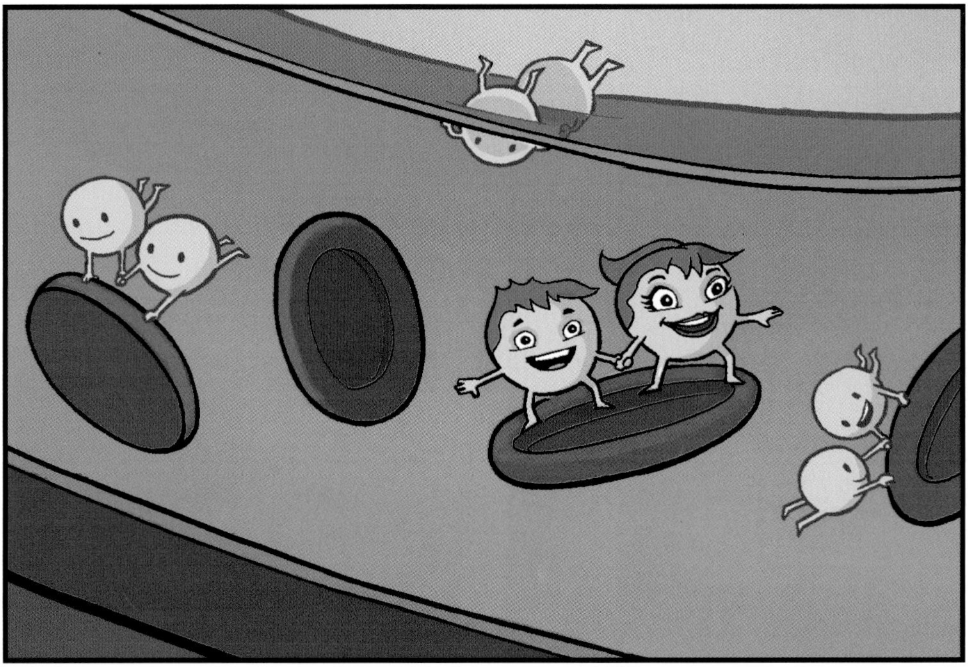

Then the blood and oxygen travel to the heart.

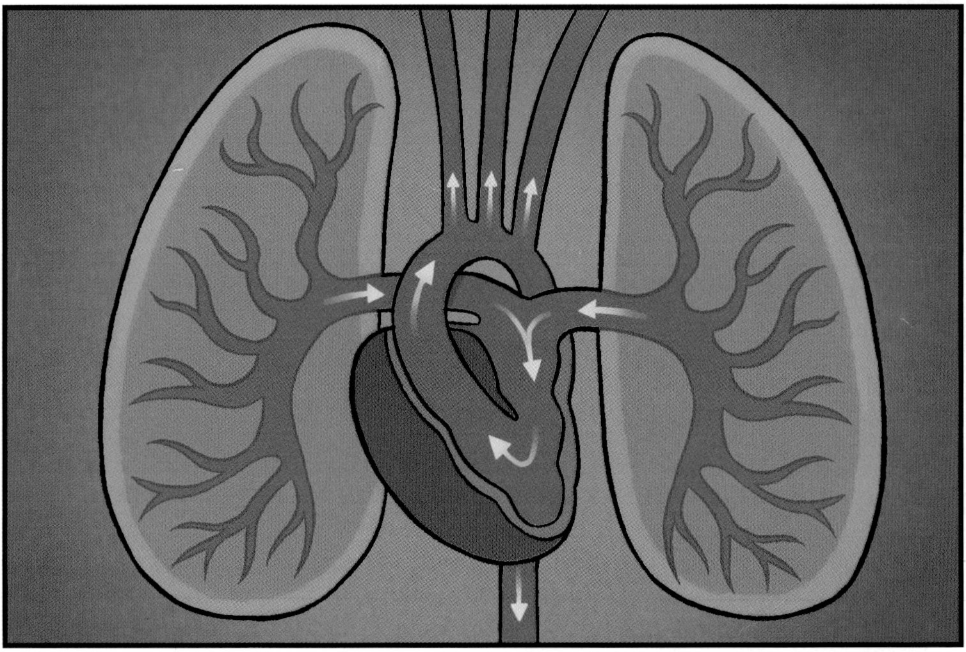

The heart pumps blood and oxygen to every part of your body.

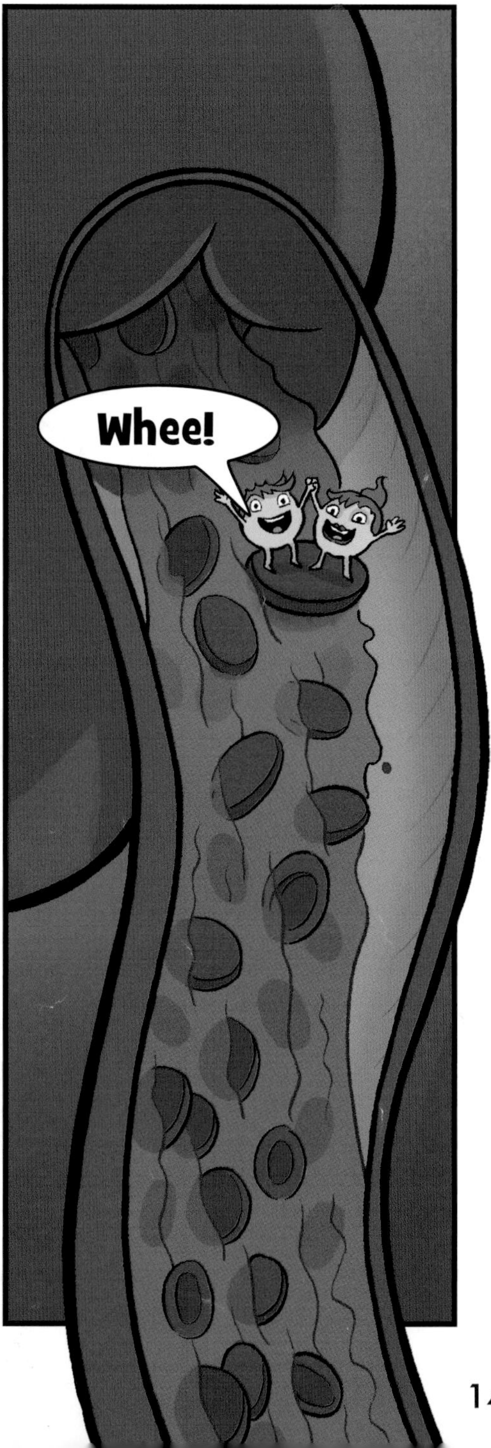
Whee!

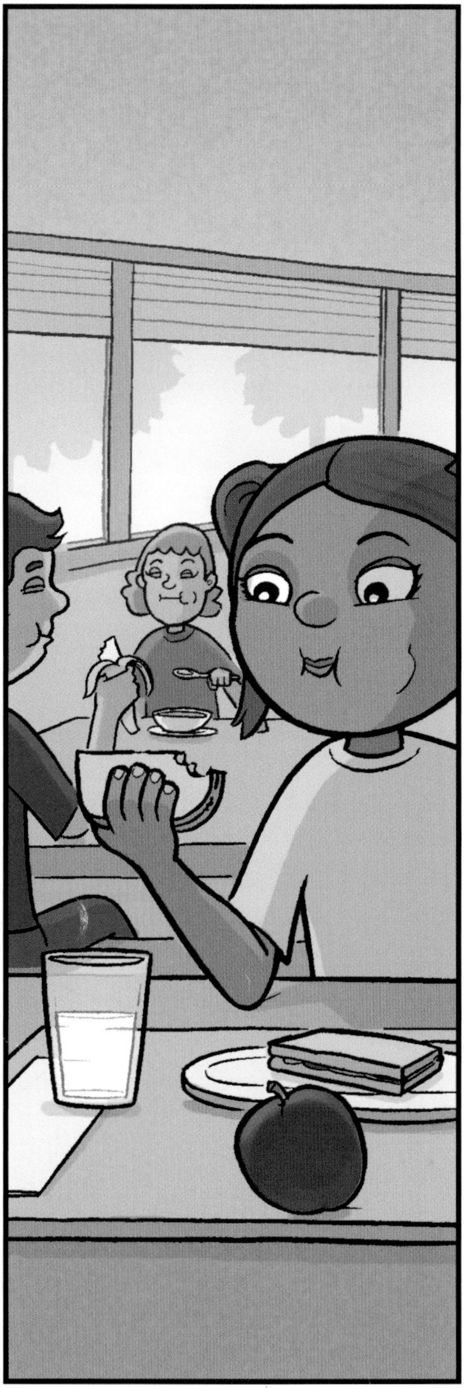

Oxygen helps change food into energy.

You need energy for everything you do.

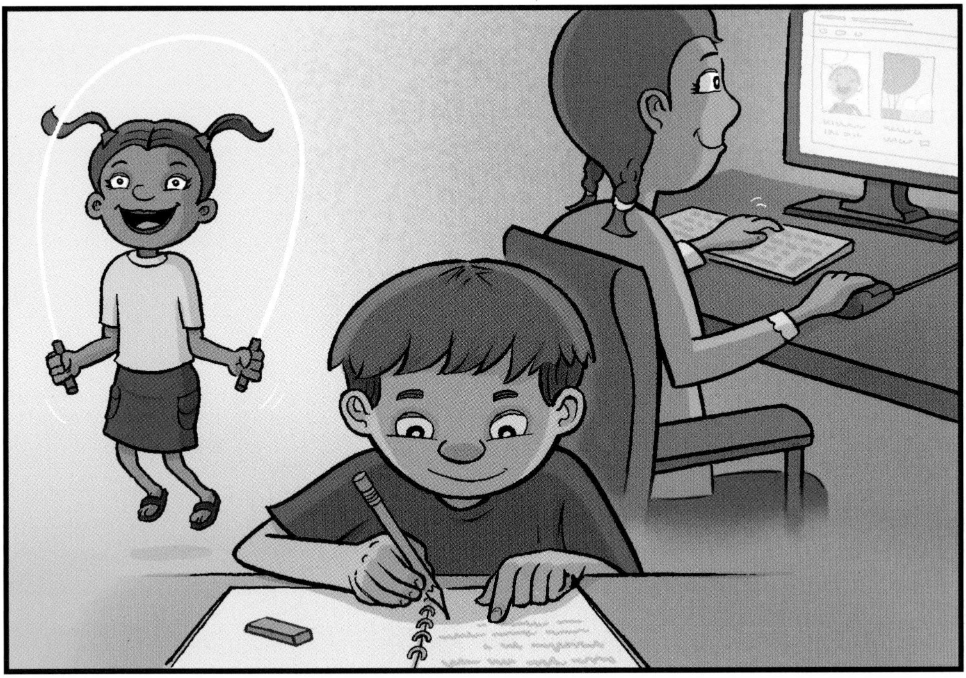

With all that activity, your body makes carbon dioxide gas.

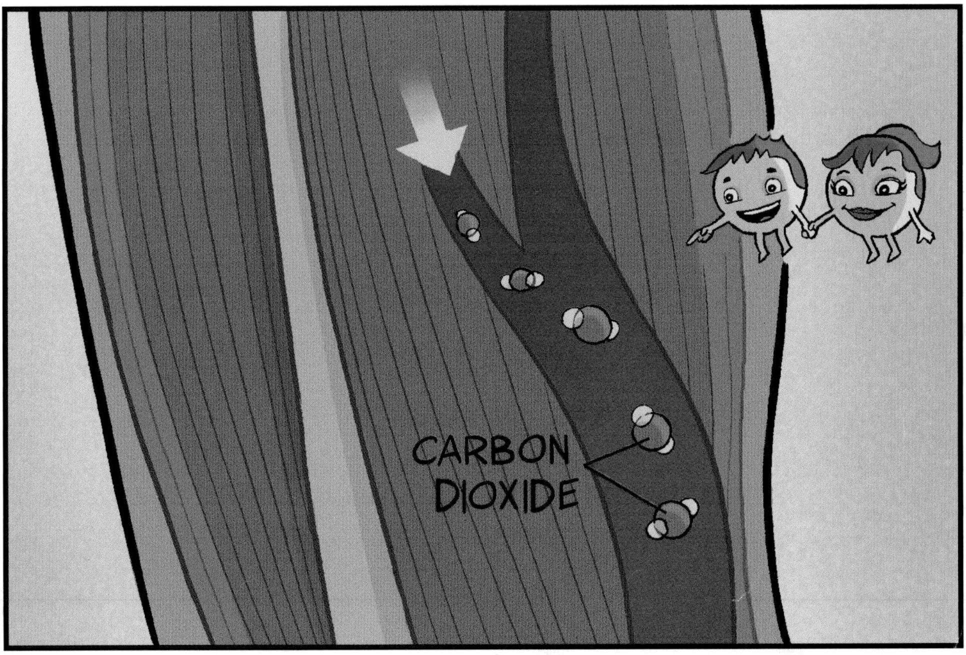
CARBON
DIOXIDE

Letting It All Out

To stay healthy, your body needs to get rid of carbon dioxide.

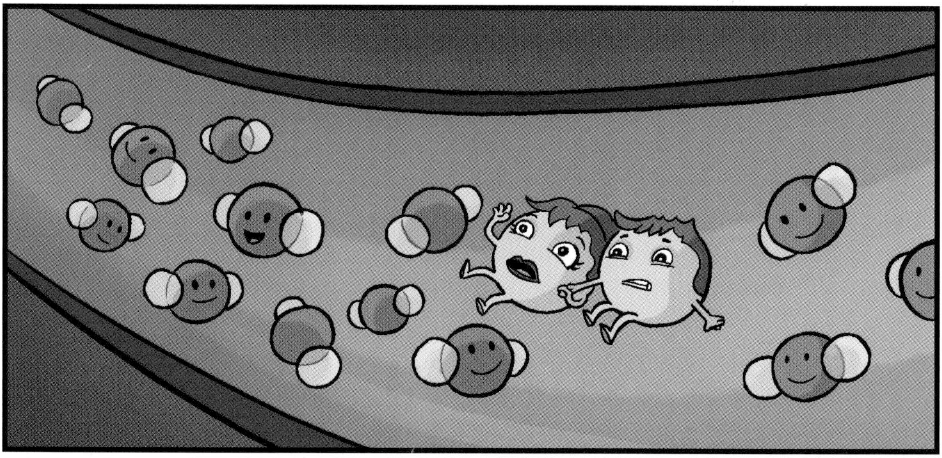

Your blood takes carbon dioxide back to the heart and lungs.

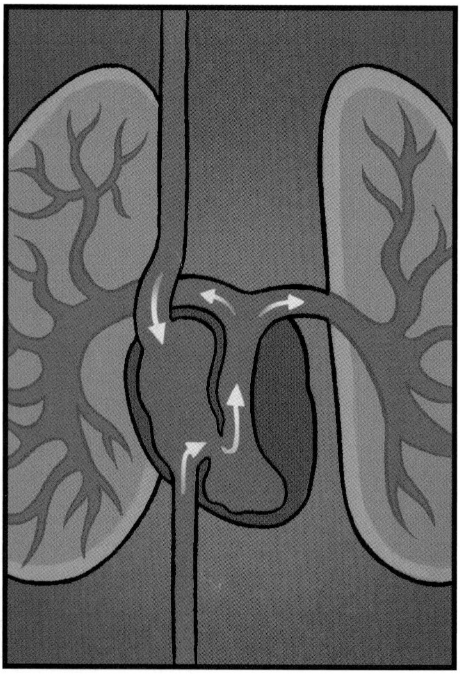

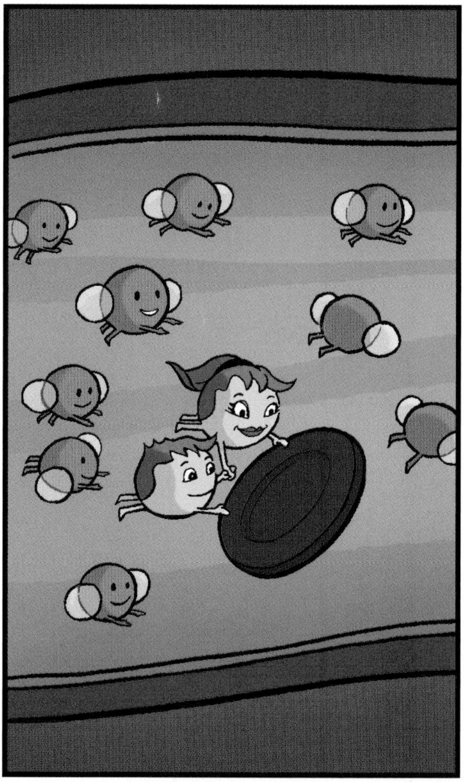

It travels to the capillaries.

Carbon dioxide and extra oxygen slip into the air sacs.

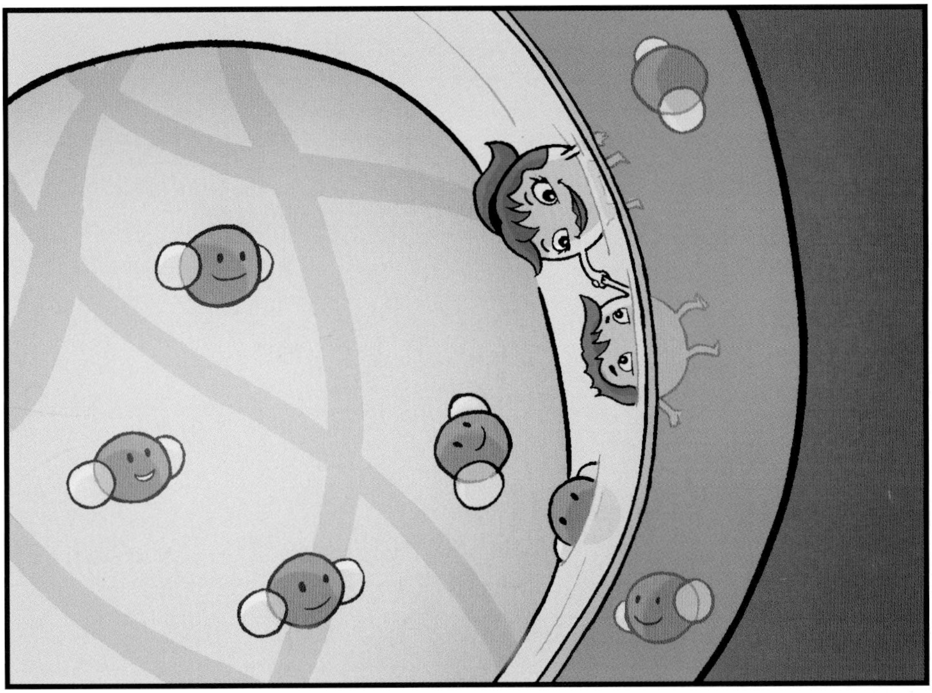

As carbon dioxide moves out of the blood, oxygen moves into it.

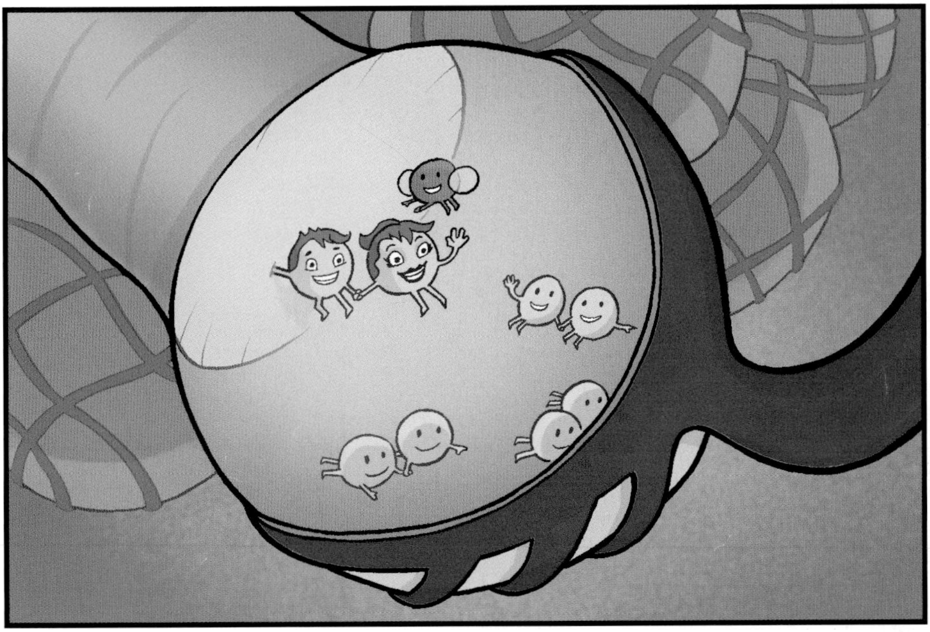

Your diaphragm relaxes. Carbon dioxide is squeezed out of your lungs.

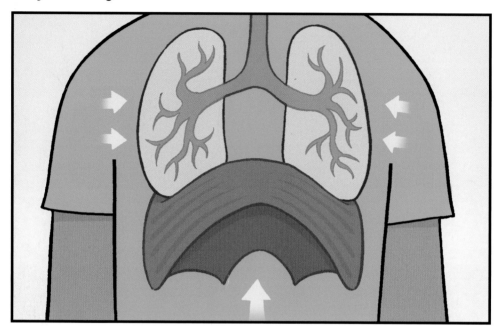

Carbon dioxide gas rushes into the bronchioles.

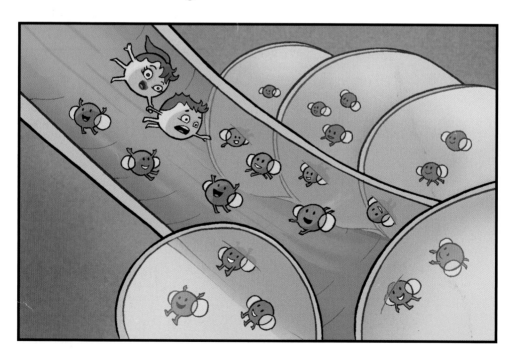

The gas moves up your trachea and throat.

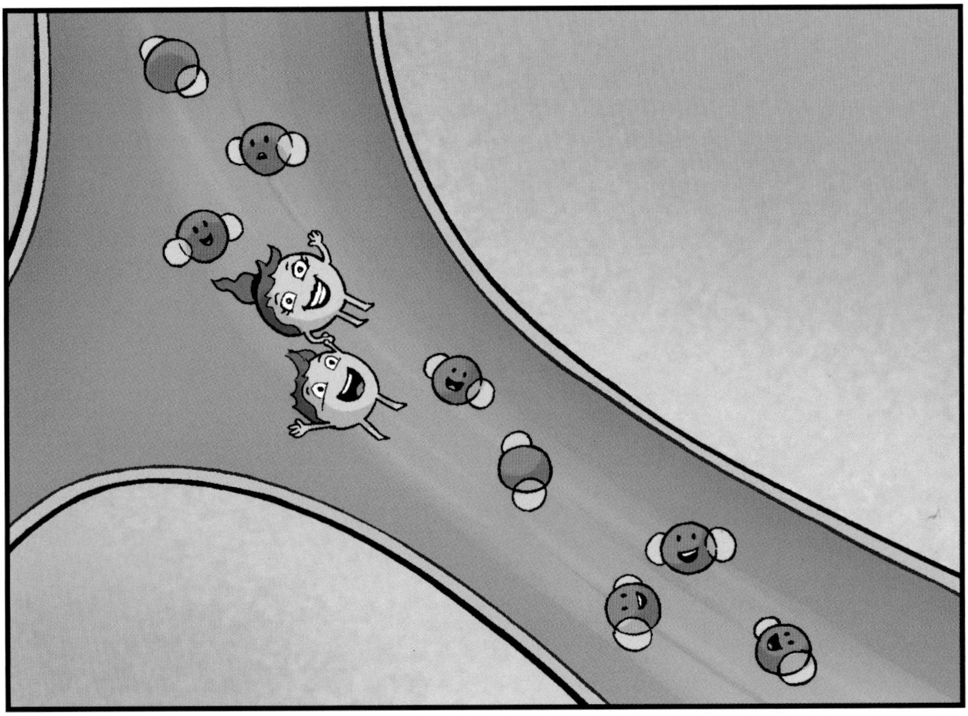

Then it escapes your body through your nose and mouth.

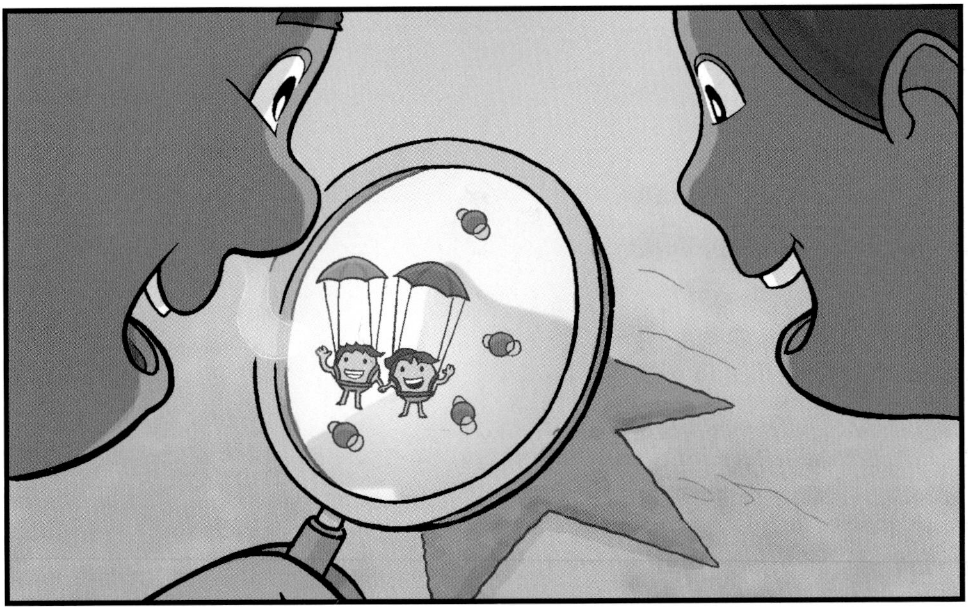

You breathe thousands of times each day.

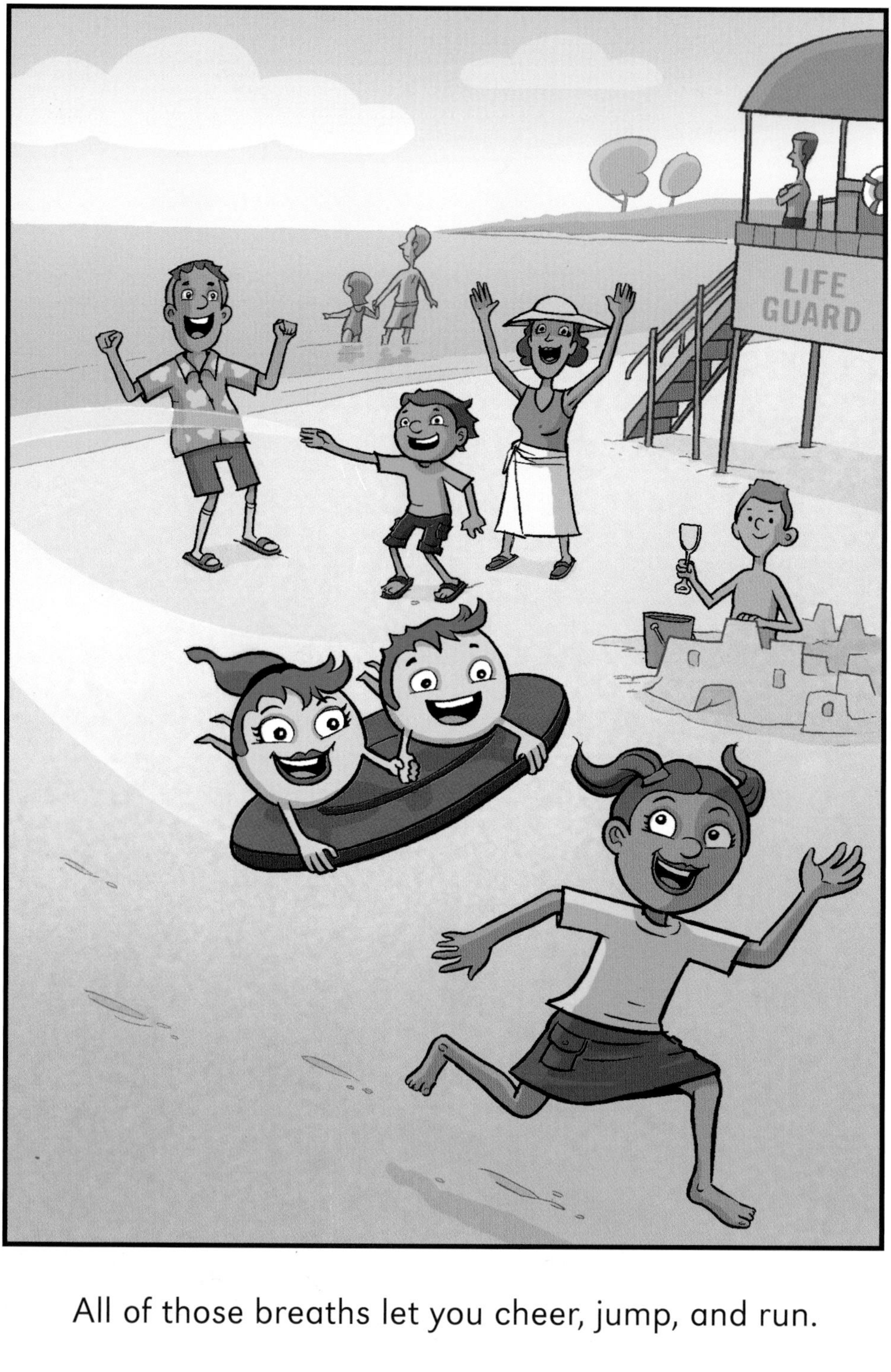
LIFE
GUARD

All of those breaths let you cheer, jump, and run.

Your respiratory system needs to stay healthy.

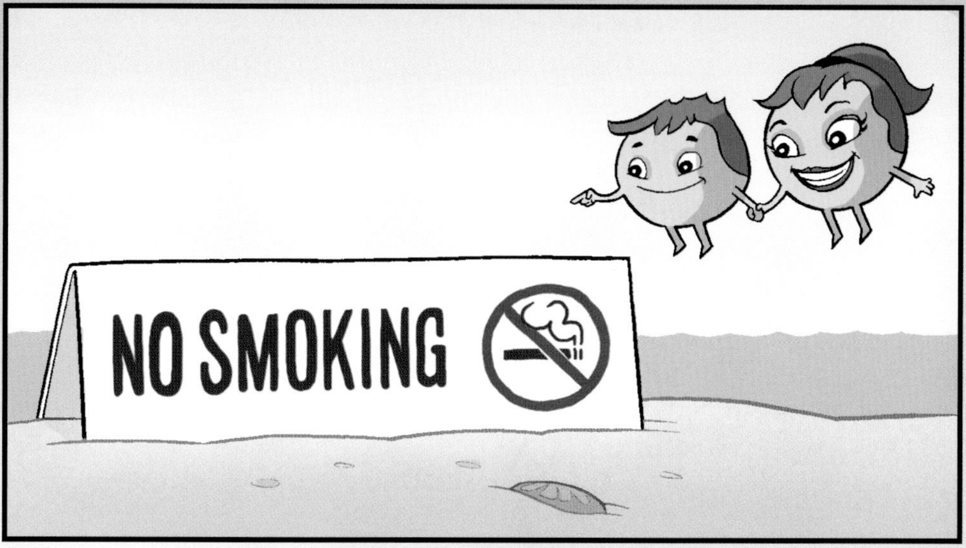
NO SMOKING

So that you can always stay active.

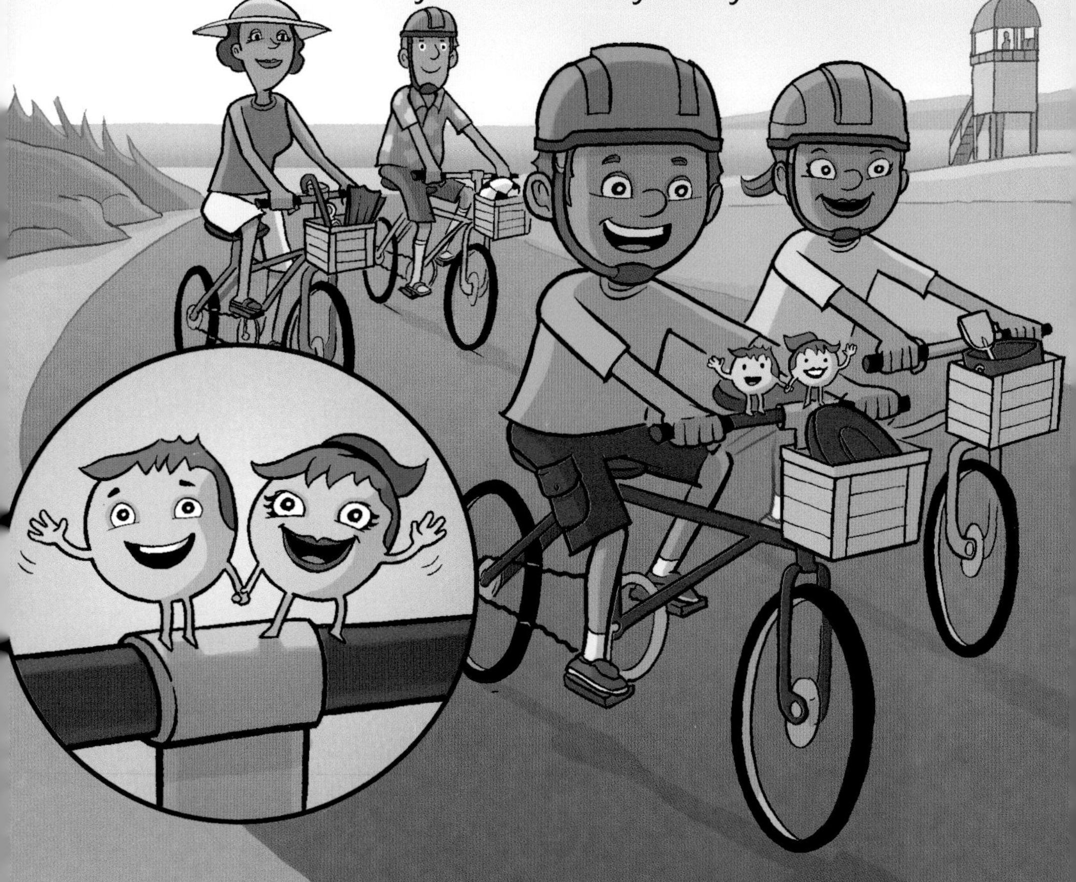

Glossary

bronchi—two airways that split from the trachea and enter the lungs

bronchioles—the smallest sections of your bronchial tubes

capillary—a small tube in your body that carries blood between the arteries and veins

carbon dioxide—a colorless, odorless gas that people and animals breathe out

cell—small, basic units of living matter

diaphragm—the muscle under your lungs that moves as you breathe

energy—the strength to do active things without getting tired

gas—something that is not solid or liquid and does not have a definite shape

oxygen—a colorless gas that people breathe; humans and animals need oxygen to live

trachea—the air passage that connects the nose and the mouth to the lungs

Read More

Guillain, Charlotte. *Our Lungs.* Our Bodies. Chicago: Heinemann Library, 2010.

Jango-Cohen, Judith. *Your Respiratory System.* How Does Your Body Work? Minneapolis: Lerner Publications Co., 2013.

Jordan, Apple. *My Lungs.* My Body. New York: Marshall Cavendish Benchmark, 2012.

Internet Sites

FactHound offers a safe, fun way to find Internet sites related to this book. All of the sites on FactHound have been researched by our staff.

Here's all you do:

Visit *www.facthound.com*

Type in this code: 9781429686525

Check out projects, games and lots more at
www.capstonekids.com

Index

Titles in this set:

A Tour of Your
Circulatory System

A Tour of Your
Digestive System

A Tour of Your
Muscular and
Skeletal Systems

A Tour of Your
Nervous System

A Tour of Your
Respiratory System